50 HIT SONGS

ALSO AVAILABLE IN THE *REALLY EASY PIANO* SERIES...

ABBA
25 GREAT HITS. ORDER NO. AM980430

BALLADS
24 CHART POP HITS. ORDER NO. AM982751

THE BEATLES
23 BEATLES HITS. ORDER NO. NO91080

CHART HITS
21 BIG CHART HITS. ORDER NO. AM993377

CHRISTMAS
24 FESTIVE CHART HITS. ORDER NO. AM980496

CLASSICAL
36 POPULAR PIECES. ORDER NO. AM980419

ELTON JOHN
24 CLASSIC SONGS. ORDER NO. AM987844

FILM SONGS
24 SCREEN HITS. ORDER NO. AM980441

FRANK SINATRA
21 CLASSIC SONGS. ORDER NO. AM987833

JAZZ
24 JAZZ CLASSICS. ORDER NO. AM982773

POP HITS
22 GREAT SONGS. ORDER NO. AM980408

SHOWSTOPPERS
24 STAGE HITS. ORDER NO. AM982784

TV HITS
25 POPULAR HITS. ORDER NO. AM985435

60s HITS
25 CLASSIC HITS. ORDER NO. AM985402

70s HITS
25 CLASSIC SONGS. ORDER NO. AM985413

80s HITS
25 POPULAR HITS. ORDER NO. AM985424

90s HITS
24 POPULAR HITS. ORDER NO. AM987811

21ST CENTURY HITS
24 POPULAR HITS. ORDER NO. AM987822

ALL TITLES CONTAIN BACKGROUND NOTES FOR EACH SONG PLUS
PLAYING TIPS AND HINTS.

PUBLISHED BY
WISE PUBLICATIONS
14-15 BERNERS STREET, LONDON, W1T 3LJ, UK.

EXCLUSIVE DISTRIBUTORS:
MUSIC SALES LIMITED
DISTRIBUTION CENTRE, NEWMARKET ROAD, BURY ST EDMUNDS,
SUFFOLK, IP33 3YB, UK.
MUSIC SALES PTY LIMITED
120 ROTHSCHILD AVENUE, ROSEBERY, NSW 2018, AUSTRALIA.

ORDER NO. AM1000615
ISBN 978-1-84938-553-4
THIS BOOK © COPYRIGHT 2010 BY WISE PUBLICATIONS,
A DIVISION OF MUSIC SALES LIMITED.

`PRINTED IN THE EU.

50 HIT SONGS

WISE PUBLICATIONS
PART OF THE MUSIC SALES GROUP
LONDON / NEW YORK / PARIS / SYDNEY / COPENHAGEN / BERLIN / MADRID / TOKYO

ALL ABOUT YOU McFLY 10

ALL THAT SHE WANTS ACE OF BASE 12

THE BARE NECESSITIES THE JUNGLE BOOK 14

BRIDGE OVER TROUBLED WATER SIMON AND GARFUNKEL 9

BYE BYE BABY (BABY GOODBYE) THE BAY CITY ROLLERS 16

CAN'T FIGHT THE MOONLIGHT LeANN RIMES 20

CAN'T TAKE MY EYES OFF YOU JERSEY BOYS 22

CANDLE IN THE WIND ELTON JOHN 18

COULD IT BE MAGIC BARRY MANILOW 26

CRAZY GNARLS BARKLEY 24

CRY ME A RIVER JUSTIN TIMBERLAKE 29

DO YOUR EARS HANG LOW TRADITIONAL 32

DO-RE-MI THE SOUND OF MUSIC 34

ETERNAL FLAME THE BANGLES 36

EVERGREEN WILL YOUNG 38

EVERY BREATH YOU TAKE THE POLICE 40

FIELDS OF GOLD STING 42

GRACE KELLY MIKA 44

HAKUNA MATATA THE LION KING 46

HEADLINES (FRIENDSHIP NEVER ENDS) SPICE GIRLS 52

HELP! THE BEATLES 54

I GOT RHYTHM GERSHWIN 56

IMAGINE JOHN LENNON 58

IT AIN'T NECESSARILY SO GERSHWIN 60

KARMA CHAMELEON CULTURE CLUB 49

LADY MADONNA THE BEATLES 62

LEAVE RIGHT NOW WILL YOUNG 64

LIVE AND LET DIE WINGS 66

LOST! COLDPLAY 67

A MOMENT LIKE THIS LEONA LEWIS 70

MORE THAN WORDS EXTREME 72

MY BONNIE LIES OVER THE OCEAN TRADITIONAL 74

MY WAY FRANK SINATRA 76

NO MATTER WHAT WHISTLE DOWN THE WIND 78

OH, PRETTY WOMAN PRETTY WOMAN 80

RAINDROPS KEEP FALLING ON MY HEAD
BUTCH CASSIDY AND THE SUNDANCE KID 82

READ MY MIND THE KILLERS 84

ROCKET MAN ELTON JOHN 86

STRANGERS IN THE NIGHT FRANK SINATRA 88

SUPER TROUPER ABBA 90

SWEET DREAMS (ARE MADE OF THIS) EURYTHMICS 91

TAKE A BOW RIHANNA 92

THANK YOU FOR THE MUSIC ABBA 110

VIVA LA VIDA COLDPLAY 94

WATERLOO ABBA 98

A WHOLE NEW WORLD ALADDIN 100

WOKE UP THIS MORNING THE SOPRANOS 102

YOU'RE BEAUTIFUL JAMES BLUNT 104

YOU'RE THE ONE THAT I WANT JOHN TRAVOLTA & OLIVIA NEWTON-JOHN 105

YOU'VE GOT A FRIEND IN ME TOY STORY 108

RANK SINATRA   MIKA   ABBA   LEONA LEWIS   JOHN LENNON

ELTON JOHN   GERSHWIN   McFLY   STING   WILL YOUNG

Bridge Over Troubled Water

Words & Music by Paul Simon

This is the title track of the UK's best-selling album of the 1970s. Later on, when Paul Simon heard the appreciative applause Art Garfunkel received as lead singer, he remarked bitterly '...that's my song, man, thank you very much. I wrote that song!'

Hints & Tips: Although quite easy to play, this piece should have a dynamic climax in bars 20–21. Try to feel the whole piece building to that point and fading away after it.

All About You

Words & Music by Thomas Fletcher

McFly had their fifth hit in less than a year when this song, released as a double A-side along with their version of Carole King's classic, 'You've Got A Friend', became their third UK No. 1 in March 2005. It was that year's official Comic Relief single and was also used to promote the charity Make Poverty History.

Hints & Tips: Although a simple bass-line for the left hand, it needs to be played accurately. At bar 32 try not to rush the triplet, keep it even.

All That She Wants

Words & Music by Buddha & Joker

Swedish pop group Ace Of Base reached No. 1 in the UK charts in 1993 with this single.
It was produced by the legendary Denniz Pop and taken from their debut album *Happy Nation*.

Hints & Tips: Practise the introduction (the first four bars) of this song slowly to ensure both
the left hand and right hand are moving from note to note at exactly the same time.

The Bare Necessities

Music by Terry Gilkyson

Baloo the bear meets the man cub, Mowgli, and gets him to loosen up a little and go with the flow in this song from the Disney story adapted from Rudyard Kipling's book.

Hints & Tips: Follow the words of the song to help you with the tied rhythms. Make this piece bouncy and bright by playing staccato. 2/2 means two beats in the bar, but it's best to count four, and play much slower, until you know the music.

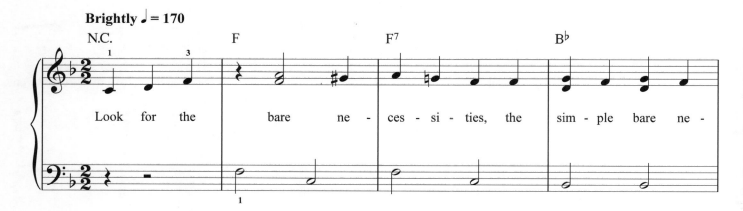

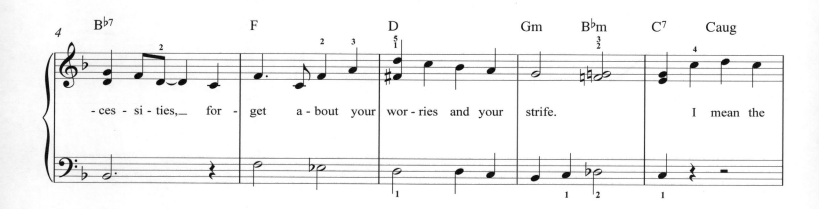

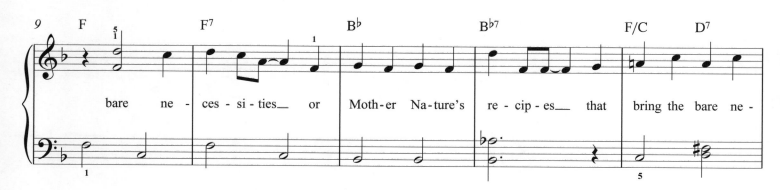

-ces - si - ties___ of life. Wher-ev - er I wan - der,___

___ wher-ev-er I roam,___ I could-n't be fon - der___ of my big

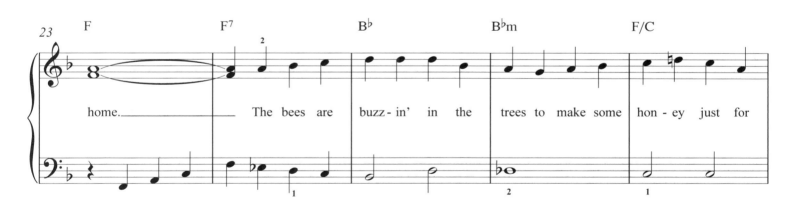

home.___ The bees are buzz-in' in the trees to make some hon-ey just for

me. The bare ne - ces - si-ties of life will come to you.___

Bye Bye Baby (Baby Goodbye)

Words & Music by Bob Crewe & Bob Gaudio

The successful writing partnership of Bob Crewe and Bob Gaudio brought many hits for American pop artists.
This song was first recorded by The Four Seasons (of whom Gaudio was a member) and in 1965 it reached US No. 12.
Ten years later The Bay City Rollers recorded a version which sold a million copies and reached No. 1!

Hints & Tips: Watch out for the key changes in bars 9, 23 and 31.
Make sure you know which notes are naturals, sharps and flats, in each key.

why beg — in it? 'Cause there ain't an — y fut — ure in it. She's got me and

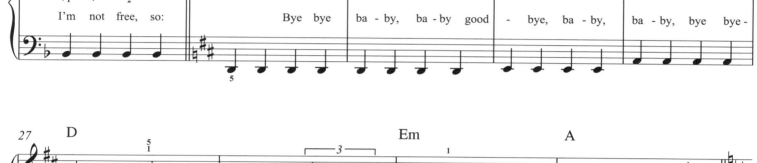

I'm not free, so: Bye bye ba — by, ba — by good — bye, ba — by, ba — by, bye bye-

- aye. Bye bye ba — by, don't make me cry, ba — by, ba — by, bye bye.

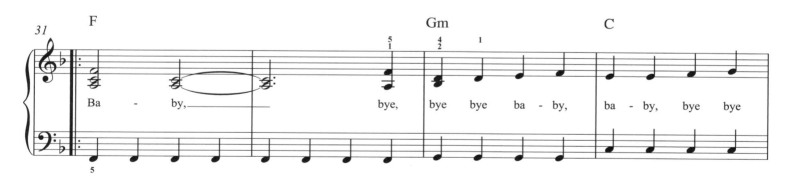

Ba — by, bye, bye bye ba — by, ba — by, bye bye

ba — by, bye bye cry ba — by, ba — by, bye bye.

Candle In The Wind

Words & Music by Elton John & Bernie Taupin

'Candle in the Wind' was originally released in 1973 having been written in honour of Marilyn Monroe. In 1997 Elton John reworked the song as a tribute to Diana, Princess of Wales. It sold over 600,000 copies on its first day of release and became the best-selling single of all time in the UK.

Hints & Tips: Don't be late with the left hand where it plays alone e.g. bars 7, 15 and 24. Also, try and work out where the beats fall in the syncopated bars. This will help you to understand the rhythm more clearly.

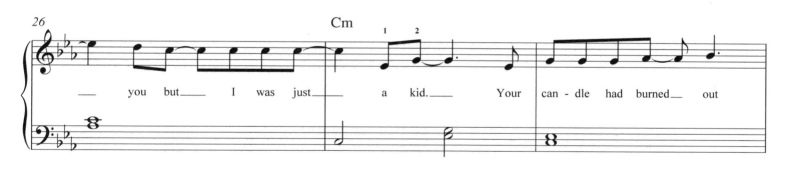

FROM 'COYOTE UGLY'

Can't Fight The Moonlight

Words & Music by Diane Warren

This is one of four songs performed by country star LeAnn Rimes for the character Violet, a would-be songwriter who goes to New York to pursue her dreams and gets a job as a barmaid at the Coyote Ugly Saloon. Rimes has a cameo role in the film, effectively duetting with herself!

Hints & Tips: Don't be put off by the fact that the words you would naturally emphasise often fall on the weak beats of the bar, rather than the strong beats as you would usually expect. Playing it slowly at first might help you keep your wits about you.

Can't Take My Eyes Off You

Words & Music by Bob Crewe & Bob Gaudio

This documentary-style musical, which opened on Broadway in November 2005 and at London's Prince Edward Theatre in February 2008, tells the turbulent story of the rise to fame of Frankie Valli and The Four Seasons, although this song from 1967 was one of several hits that Valli recorded without the group.

Hints & Tips: Be sure to hold the tied semibreves (whole notes) in the left hand for their full value. Keep the rhythm very steady.

GNARLS BARKLEY

Crazy

Words & Music by Thomas Callaway, Brian Burton, Gianfranco Reverberi & Gian Piero Reverberi

DJ/producer Danger Mouse and rapper/singer Cee-Lo (a.k.a. Gnarls Barkley) made history in March 2006 when 'Crazy' became the first ever single to top the UK singles chart on download sales alone, having been released online a week prior to its release as a CD single.

Hints & Tips: Practise this piece slowly at first, paying careful attention to the fingerings. If your hand cannot stretch to the octave spread required in bars 16–21 just play the top notes starting with your thumb on the C.

BARRY MANILOW

Could It Be Magic

Words & Music by Barry Manilow & Adrienne Anderson

This song is based on Chopin's 'Prelude in C Minor, Op. 28, No. 20'. It was a very successful single from Barry Manilow's first album in 1975. It was subsequently a hit for Donna Summer and Take That.

Hints & Tips: If you look carefully at the chorale-like chords at the beginning and compare them to the harmonies of the chorus, you will notice they are very similar. Barry Manilow has taken the harmonic structure and embellished Chopin's melody to create a new piece of music.

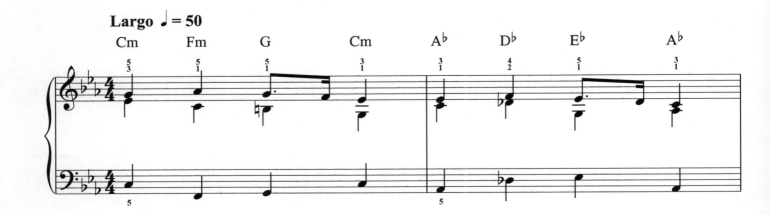

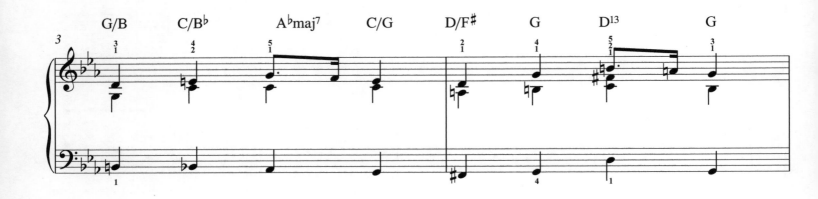

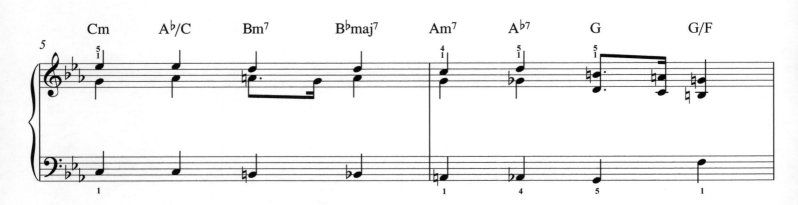

Cry Me A River

Words & Music by Justin Timberlake, Scott Storch & Tim Mosley

'Cry Me A River' was recorded by Justin Timberlake and charted at No. 2 in February 2003, remaining in the charts for a further 12 weeks. Justin was born on 31 January, 1981 in Memphis, Tennessee and started his show-biz career as a 'Mousekateer' on the Mickey Mouse Club—a US children's show. He was catapulted into the dizzy heights of fame when he joined teeny-pop boy band *NSYNC, which paved the way towards his hugely successful solo career as we know it.

Hints & Tips: Some of the rhythms are pretty tricky here, so practise the right hand on its own. It may help if you mark the beats by tapping with your left hand or foot.

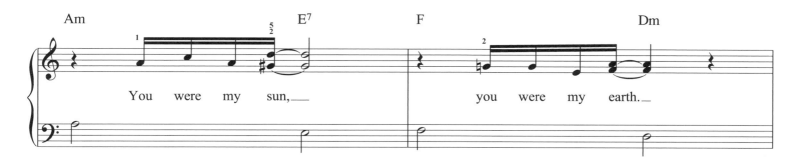

and made oth - er plans.___ But I bet you did - n't think that they would come crash -

- ing down, no. You don't have to say what you did. I

al - rea - dy know I found out from him. Now there's just no chance for you and me, there'll

nev - er be and don't it make you sad a - bout it? Told me you love___ me, why did you leave___

___ me all a - lone? Now you tell me you need___ me when you call me on the phone.

Girl, I re - fuse,_ you must have me con - fused with some oth - er guy._

Your brid - ges were burned,_ now it's your turn_ to cry. Cry me a riv -

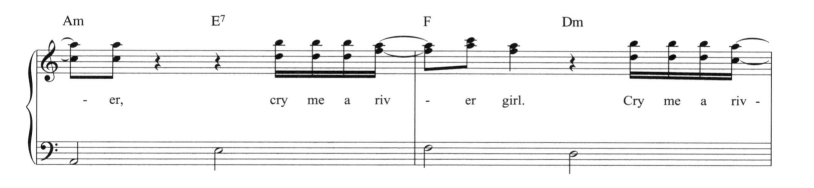

- er, cry me a riv - er girl. Cry me a riv -

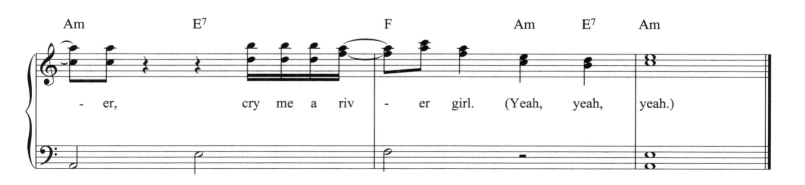

- er, cry me a riv - er girl. (Yeah, yeah, yeah.)

Do Your Ears Hang Low

Traditional

There are several theories as to the origin of the various versions of this song, most of which have a military connection and are too rude to mention here! However it is a song often sung by children, either in schools or at camps, and when used in the 1980s TV series Kidsongs, was thought to refer to a basset hound.

Hints & Tips: Aim to be rhythmic with this piece, rather than fast. Once a piece is learned properly it can be sped up, it is far more difficult and ultimately detrimental to one's technique to approach a piece in too much haste.

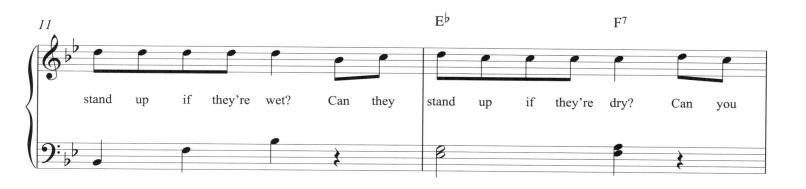

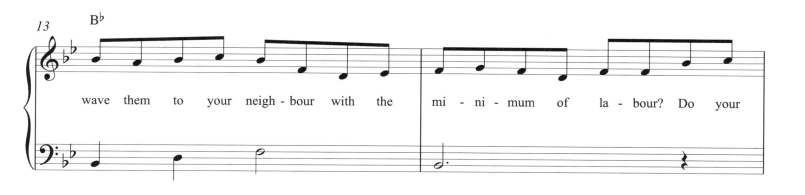

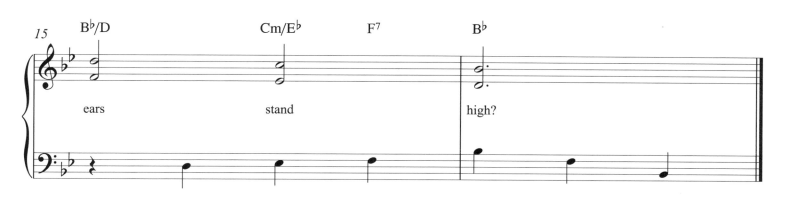

Do-Re-Mi

Words by Oscar Hammerstein II • Music by Richard Rodgers

This was the last musical written by Rodgers and Hammerstein as the latter died soon after its Broadway premiere in 1959. Shortly after being introduced to the Von Trapp children their governess, Maria, uses this song to teach them the notes of the musical scale as they learn to sing.

Hints & Tips: Rock gently between the two notes in the introduction if your left hand cannot reach to an octave. Keep your wrist loose and your touch light. If you're struggling omit the higher note.

35

Eternal Flame

Words & Music by Susanna Hoffs, Tom Kelly & Billy Steinberg

The Bangles' lead singer Susanna Hoffs was keen to write a ballad that would not have been out of place on the Beatles' album, *Revolver*. 'Eternal Flame', with its double bridge structure and lack of chorus, was the result.

Hints & Tips: The rhythm of the melody is quite tricky. If it helps, write out the beats above the right hand. Also, watch out for the accidentals from bar 19 to the end.

Evergreen

Words & Music by Jorgen Elofsson, Per Magnusson & David Kreuger

Having seen off competition in the form of Gareth Gates, Will Young, the winner of Pop Idol 2002, broke first-day sales records with this, his debut single.

Hints & Tips: Although it is not mentioned in the music, you could try to make the difference in character between the verse and chorus clear. The chorus (which starts in bar 15) can be played louder and more jubilantly whilst the verse can be more understated.

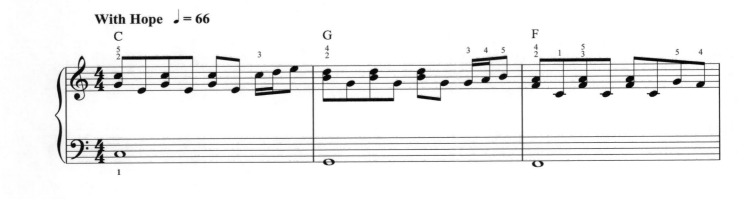

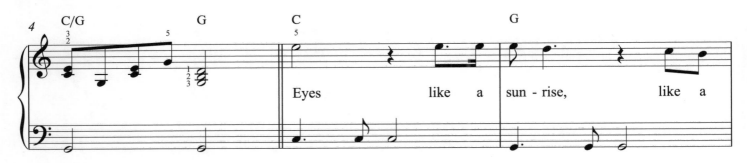

Eyes like a sun - rise, like a

rain - fall down___ my soul. And I won - der,___ I won - der why you

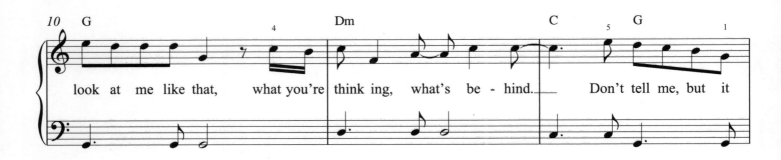

look at me like that, what you're think ing, what's be - hind. Don't tell me, but it

Every Breath You Take

Words & Music by Sting

Those who classify this as a love song have probably not listened closely to the lyrics. It was written as Sting's first marriage to Francis Tomelty was breaking up, and concerns the actions of an obsessive stalker, who is watching 'every move you make'.

Hints & Tips: The left-hand riff is not identical to the record, as the original riff is more suited to a guitar. However, try to give it the same hypnotic and repetitive feel.

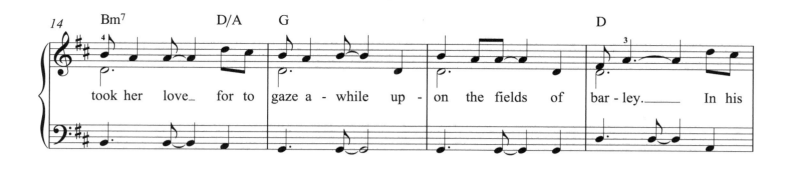

took her love_ for to gaze a - while up - on the fields of bar - ley._____ In his

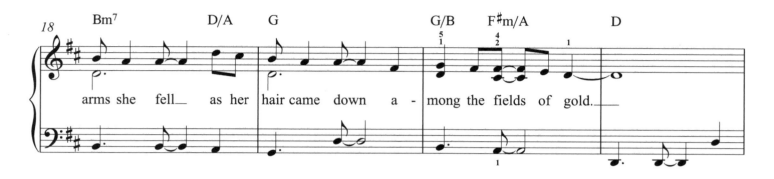

arms she fell_ as her hair came down a - mong the fields of gold._

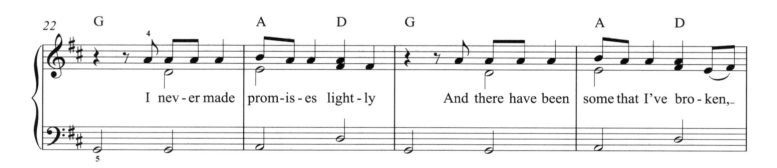

I nev - er made prom - is - es light - ly   And there have been   some that I've bro - ken,_

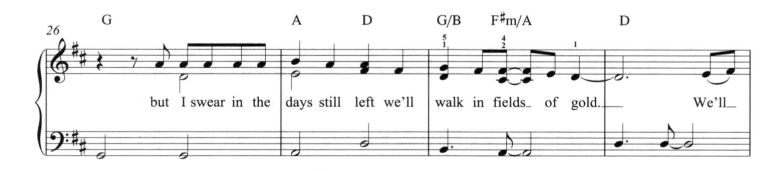

but I swear in the   days still left we'll   walk in fields_ of gold._   We'll_

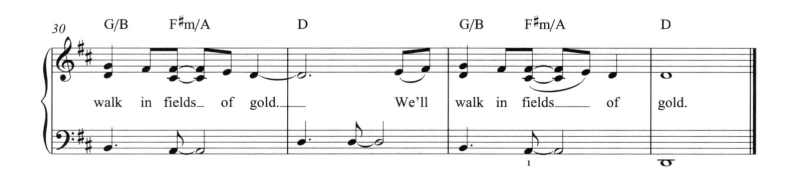

walk in fields_ of gold._____   We'll   walk in fields_____ of   gold.

MIKA

Grace Kelly

Words & Music by Mika, Jodi Marr, Dan Warner & John Merchant

Meant as a mocking satire of musicians who reinvent themselves in order to be popular, this song by Beirut-born Mika, which includes references to Rossini's opera The Barber of Seville, became only the second to reach No. 1 on downloads alone when it topped the UK charts for five weeks from late January 2007 onwards.

Hints & Tips: The first thing to notice about this song is the swing rhythm, so all quavers are divided as indicated after the metronome marking. Secondly, there are many groups of triplets, so take care that they are played rhythmically and even.

Hakuna Matata

Words by Tim Rice • Music by Elton John

The title of this song, one of three from the Disney movie The Lion King to be nominated in 1995 for an Academy Award, is a Swahili phrase which means 'no worries' or 'no problem'. It is sung by Timon, a meerkat, and Pumbaa, a warthog, as they try to convince the lion cub Simba to forget his troubled past.

Hints & Tips: The opening to this song is like a recitative, a style of speech-like singing, usually found in operas between songs, telling the story, and not always particularly rhythmic. Here it would be wise to keep it rhythmic for the sake of learning the notes, afterwhich you may like to play with more freedom, as if they were being spoken.

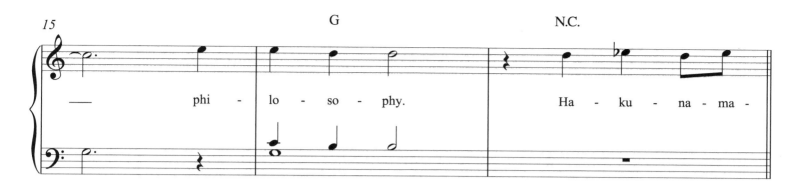

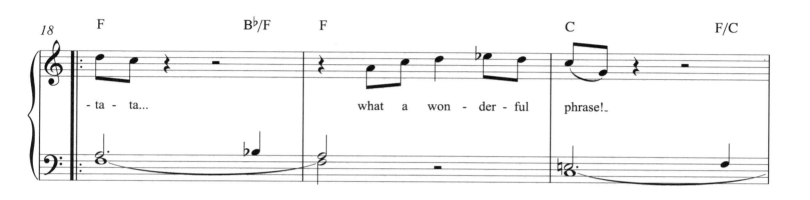

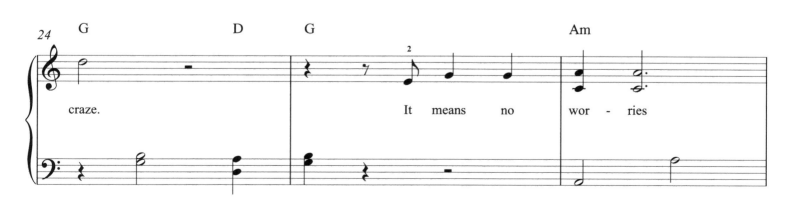

47

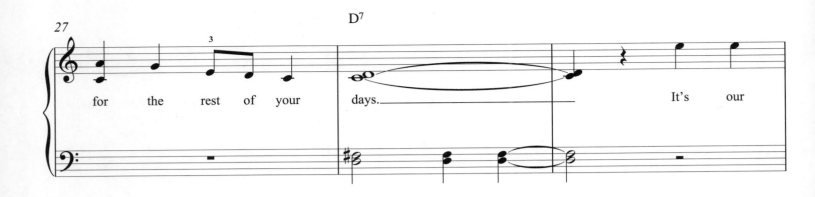

for the rest of your days._____ It's our

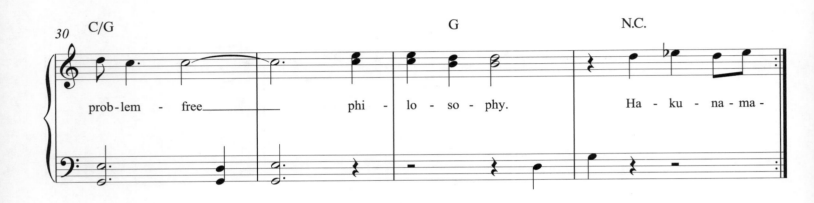

prob-lem - free_____ phi - lo - so - phy. Ha - ku - na - ma -

- ta - ta... Ha - ku - na - ma - ta - ta... Ha - ku - na - ma -

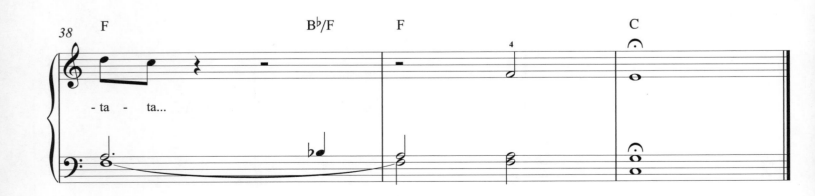

- ta - ta...

CULTURE CLUB
Karma Chameleon

Words & Music by George O'Dowd, Jonathan Moss, Roy Hay, Michael Craig & Philip Pickett

This was Culture Club's biggest hit, reaching No. 1 in both the UK and the US. In June 2006, the band was trying to recruit (via an obscure internet site) a new lead singer for a 2007 world tour and TV series!

Hints & Tips: Be aware that the bass riff in the left hand at the beginning is very repetitive, and therefore not as tricky as it looks. Notice how it is repeated at different pitches.

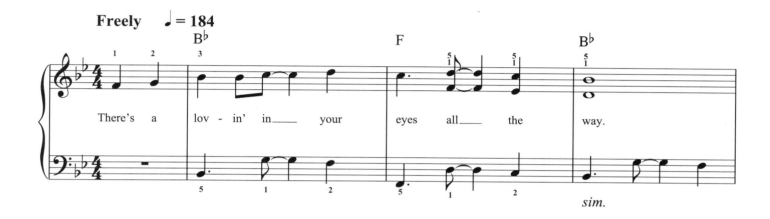

There's a lov - in' in___ your eyes all___ the way.

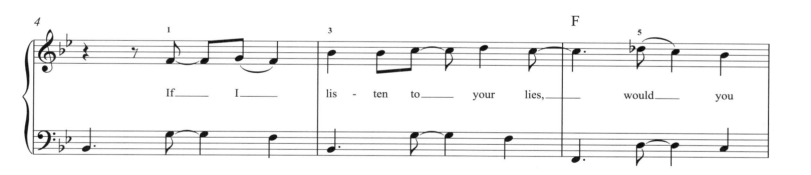

If___ I___ lis - ten to___ your lies,___ would___ you

say? I'm___ a man

with - out___ con - vic - tion.___ I'm___ a man___

who does - n't know how___ to sell___

a con - tra - dic - tion.___ You come___ and go;

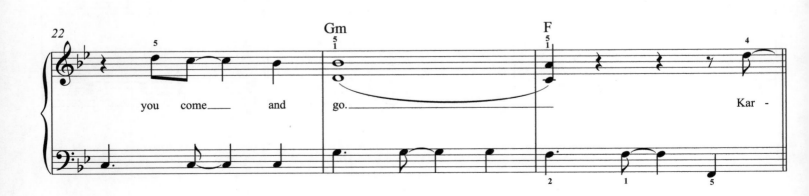

you come___ and go.___ Kar -

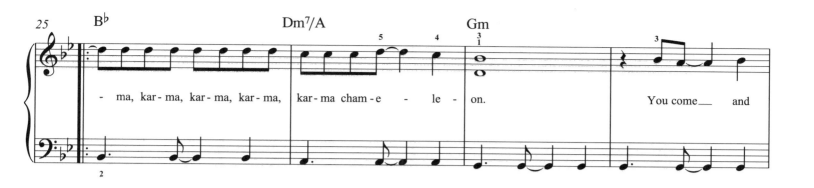

-ma, kar-ma, kar-ma, kar-ma, kar-ma cham-e - le - on. You come___ and

go; you come___ and go.___

Lov-ing would be eas-y if your col-ours were like___ my___ dreams; red, gold and

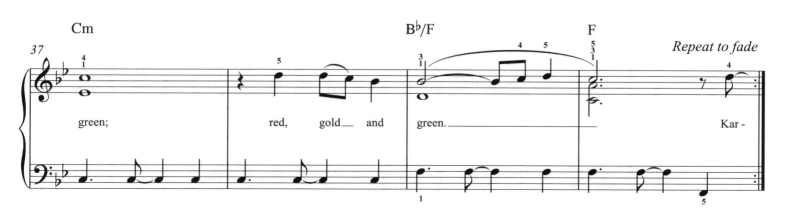

green; red, gold___ and green.___ Kar-

Repeat to fade

Headlines (Friendship Never Ends)

Words & Music by Emma Bunton, Geri Halliwell, Victoria Beckham, Melanie Chisholm, Matt Rowe, Richard Stannard & Melanie Brown

Following the band's decision to reunite, this was the Spice Girls' first single featuring the original line-up since Geri Halliwell left in 1998. Taken from their *Greatest Hits* compilation album, and selected as the official Children In Need single of 2007, the band performed it for the telethon, appearing live from Los Angeles.

Hints & Tips: The trickiest bar in this piece is probably bar 24, in which the left hand takes over the melody. Practise this slowly, keeping your fingers close to the keys and trying to play it as smoothly as possible.

Help!

Words & Music by John Lennon & Paul McCartney

Also the title of the Beatles' second feature film, 'Help!' is considered to be the first Beatles song not written about love. The lyrics reflect the unrelenting pressure of fame that now bore down upon them. This would eventually lead to the band stopping playing live concerts altogether.

Hints & Tips: Watch out for the tied notes in the melody. If you sing the words whilst playing the piano, you may find it easier to get the rhythm right.

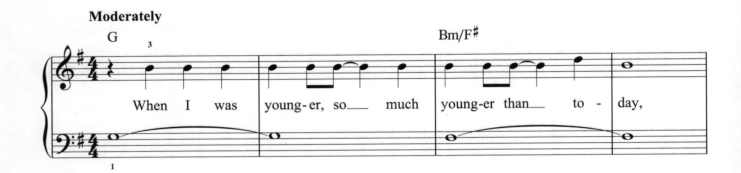

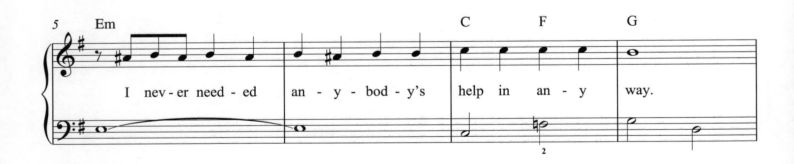

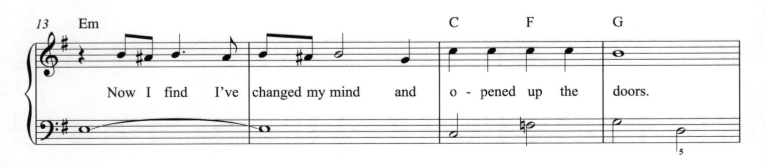

Help me if you can I'm feel - ing down, _____ and I

do ap - prec - i - ate you be - ing round. _____

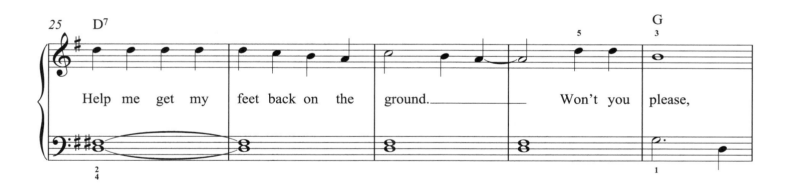

Help me get my feet back on the ground. _____ Won't you please,

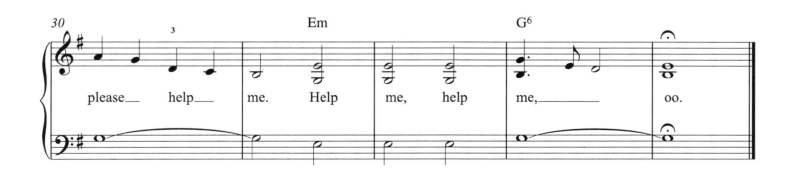

please ___ help ___ me. Help me, help me, _____ oo.

I Got Rhythm

Music by George Gershwin

The chord progression of this widely-recorded jazz standard from the musical Girl Crazy forms the basis of many other popular jazz tunes. Later expanded and used as the theme of Gershwin's final concert piece, the melody uses four notes of the pentatonic scale, first rising and then falling.

Hints & Tips: This is a fast piece with a complex, syncopated rhythm, typical of Gershwin. Pay particular attention to the suggested fingering as it will help you to play more accurately at a faster pace.

JOHN LENNON

Imagine

Words & Music by John Lennon

In 2000, George Michael paid two million dollars for the small upright piano this utopian, idealistic song had been composed on. The song was re-released in 1980 after John Lennon's death. It reached No. 1 and was only eventually replaced by John Lennon's 'Woman'.

Hints & Tips: Try to listen to a recording of this song if you find the rhythms tricky. The rhythms that John Lennon sings are vocally quite natural, but pianistically quite difficult!

It Ain't Necessarily So

Music by George Gershwin

Porgy and Bess, conceived as an American folk opera, featured an entire cast of classically-trained African-American singers, a daring and visionary artistic choice at the time. The character Sportin' Life, a drug dealer, sings this number, expressing his doubt about statements in the Bible.

Hints & Tips: Keep the triplets evenly spaced throughout the piece. Commonly the first two notes are held for too long and the last cut short; counteract this by practising with a metronome.

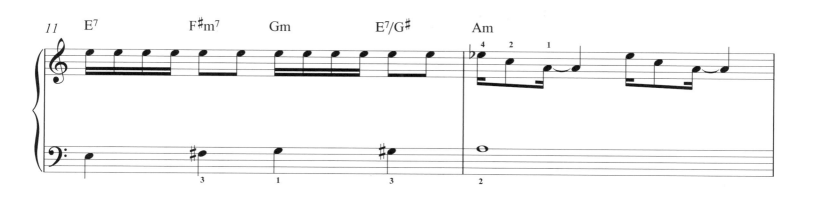

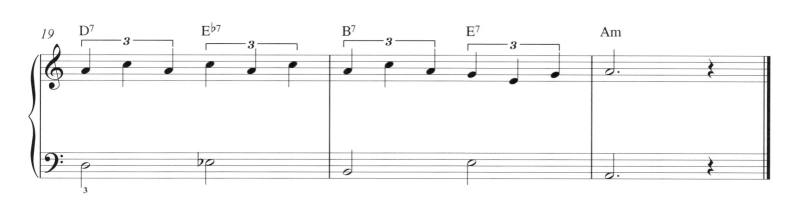

Lady Madonna

Words & Music by John Lennon & Paul McCartney

Supposedly inspired by a Humphrey Lyttleton jazz classic, 'Bad Penny Blues', 'Lady Madonna' went to No. 1 on 27 March 1968 and was the band's 14th No. 1 hit. It features the group blowing through cupped hands to imitate a brass section.

Hints & Tips: This piece should be rhythmically sharp throughout. Pay special attention to the staccato dots; the left hand in bars 23 and 24 is a good example. Try to make the staccato notes as short as possible to distinguish them from the other, longer notes.

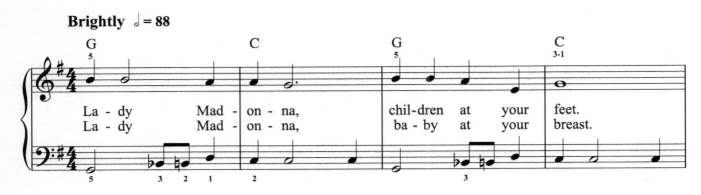

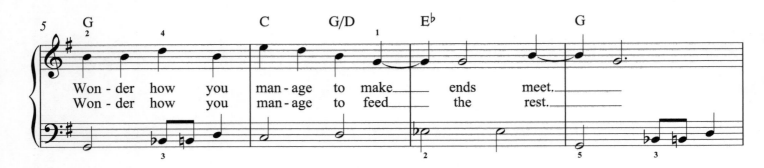

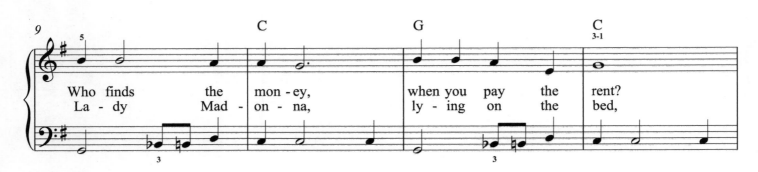

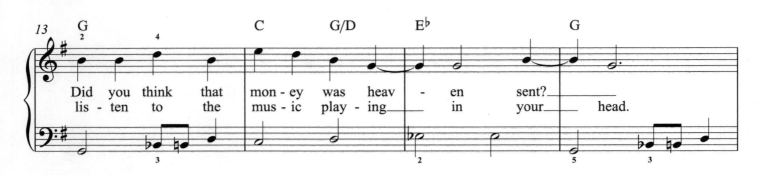

Leave Right Now

Words & Music by Eg White

According to Will Young, the first UK Pop Idol, this is 'a classically sad song about what your heart and your head says'. It was his fourth UK No. 1 single and the first to be taken from his second album, *Friday's Child*. It won the 2004 Ivor Novello Award for Best Song, Musically and Lyrically, for composer Francis 'Eg' White.

Hints & Tips: There are several groups of repeated notes in the right hand in the chorus. Keep these light and place a slight emphasis on those notes which fall on the crotchet beats within each bar to give the melody line a sense of shape.

Live And Let Die

Words & Music by Paul & Linda McCartney

Paul McCartney's band, Wings, was a natural choice for this 1973 Roger Moore Bond film theme tune. In the view of most ardent Bond fans, this song—a Grammy winner orchestrated by George Martin—is equal in quality to 'Goldfinger'.

Hints & Tips: It's almost certainly worth practising this piece hands separately to start with. Make sure you hold all the left-hand notes for their full value.

Lost!

Words & Music by Guy Berryman, Chris Martin, Jon Buckland & Will Champion

Whilst the mix of 'Lost' used on the album *Viva La Vida* features church organs and handclaps, several other versions have also been released including an instrumental track and an extended version featuring a rap by Jay-Z. A vocal and piano-only rendition featured as the B-side to the single 'Violet Hill'.

Hints & Tips: The first 16 bars of this piece feature a two-bar ostinato in the left hand. Observe the suggested fingering and practise this separately before putting the right-hand melody on top.

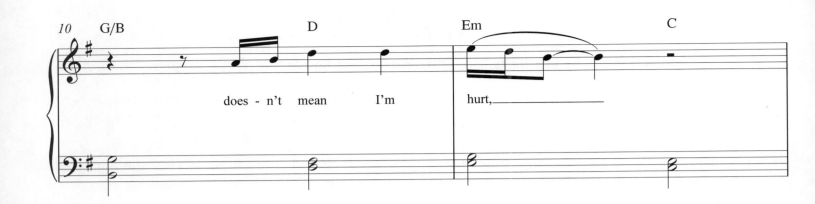

does - n't mean I'm hurt,

does - n't mean I did - n't get_____ what_ I de -

- served;__ no bet - ter and no worse._____ I just got

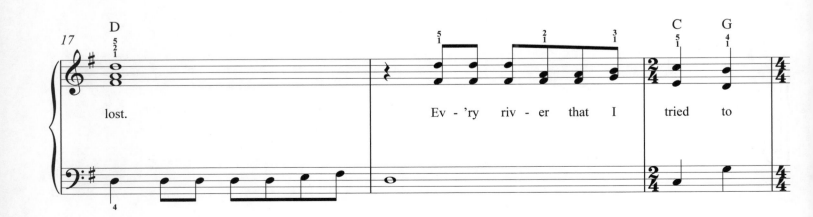

lost. Ev - 'ry riv - er that I tried to

cross,   ev - 'ry door I ev - er   tried   was

locked.   Oh,_____ and   I'm_____ just

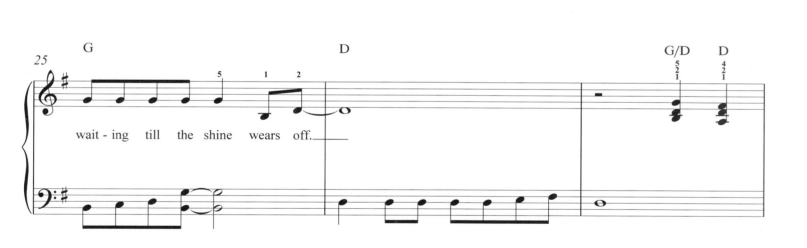

wait - ing till the shine wears off._____

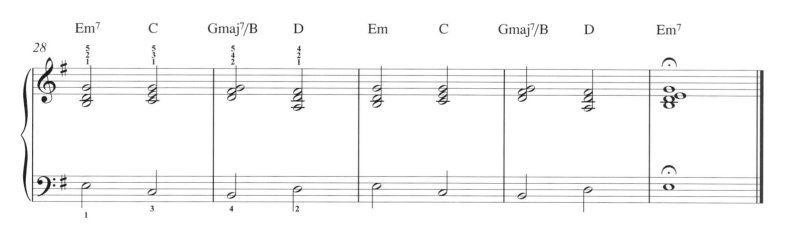

LEONA LEWIS

A Moment Like This

Words & Music by Jorgen Elofsson & John Reid

Originally recorded by Kelly Clarkson, the first winner of *American Idol*, Leona Lewis's version of this song was rush-released after she was declared the third winner of the X Factor. It debuted at No. 1 in the UK Singles Chart on 24 December 2006, making it the year's coveted Christmas No. 1 single, and stayed there for four weeks.

Hints & Tips: Be ready for the change of key at bar 11, it might sound odd at first, but learn the notes with confidence and it will soon make sense.

EXTREME
More Than Words

Words & Music by Nuno Bettencourt & Gary Cherone

Featuring intricate acoustic guitar work, this power ballad was a departure from Extreme's previous funk metal style and an incongruous inclusion on *Pornograffiti*, their 1990 concept album about a decadent and corrupt society. Usually interpreted as about emotional intimacy, it was their first mainstream success in the USA.

Hints & Tips: The melody of this piece moves off the beat more often than on it. Sub-divide the crotchet beats into two quavers in your head, or count out loud, '1 and 2 and 3 and 4 and', noting whether the note changes on a number or an 'and'. Mark this on the music too if that helps you.

My Bonnie Lies Over The Ocean

Traditional

The origin of this popular Scottish folk song remains unknown, although it is often suggested that it may refer to Charles Edward Stuart, more familiarly known as Bonnie Prince Charlie. A 1961 version recorded by Tony Sheridan featured the Beat Brothers, later to become somewhat more famous as The Beatles.

Hints & Tips: The key signature is B♭ major, so take extra care to play B♭ and E♭. The final two bars on the page are first and second time bars, which means you play through to the first time bar, repeat from the beginning, and when you reach the end for the second time play the second time bar instead of the first.

Moderately, with movement

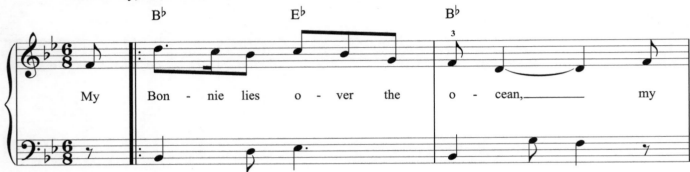

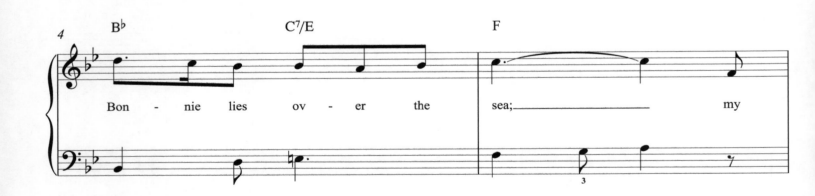

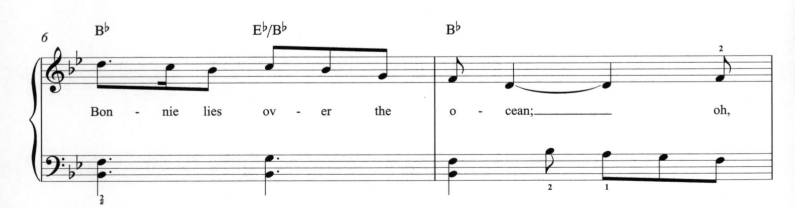

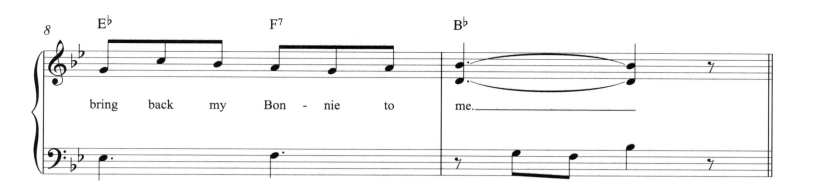

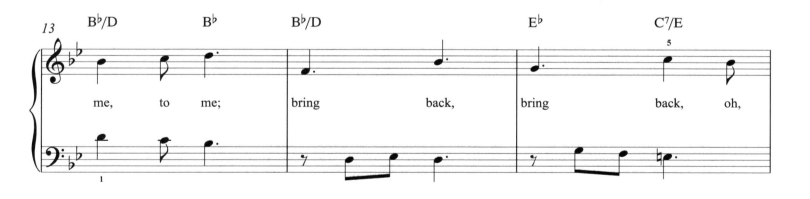

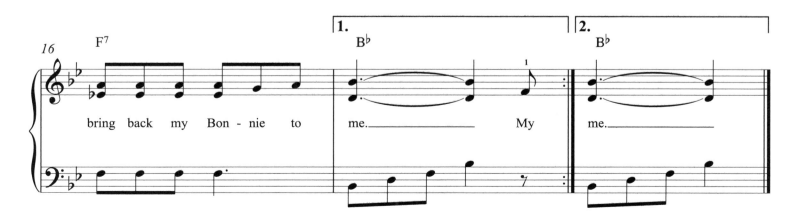

75

My Way

Words & Music by Claude Francois, Jacques Revaux & Gilles Thibaut

A millionaire songwriter and performer by the age of 20, Paul Anka bought the copyright to a French song, 'Comme d'Habitude', in 1966 and adapting it only slightly, came up with not only one of the greatest ballads of the 20th century, but the song most people identify as Frank Sinatra's signature tune.

Hints & Tips: Try starting quite softly and getting gradually louder (crescendo) through the final eight bars.

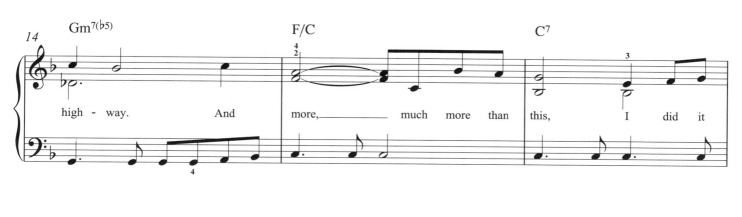

high - way. And more,_____ much more than this, I did it

my way. Yes, there were times,_____ I'm sure you knew,_____ when I bit

off more than I could chew._____ But through it all,_____ when there was

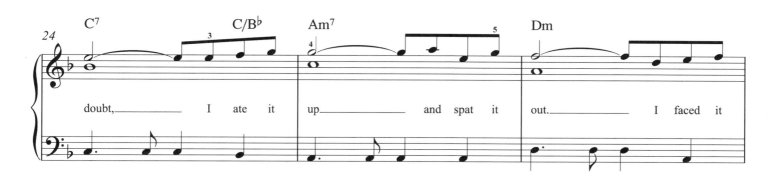

doubt,_____ I ate it up_____ and spat it out._____ I faced it

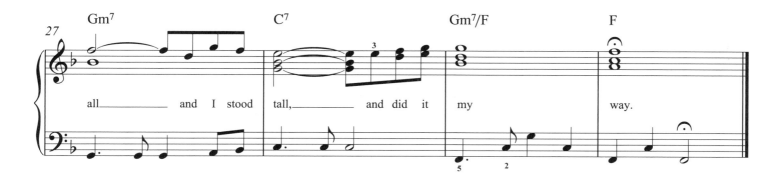

all_____ and I stood tall,_____ and did it my way.

No Matter What

Words by Jim Steinman • Music by Andrew Lloyd Webber

On 20 December 1998, one million music fans phoned ITV for this, their Record of the Year. It is taken from Andrew Lloyd Webber's successful musical, Whistle Down The Wind, and was further popularised by Boyzone.

Hints & Tips: The bass line, although less prominent than the tune in the right hand, should be played solidly and with purpose. Try to imagine the sound of a bass guitar or even a kick drum to help you.

No mat - ter where they take us, we'll find our own way back.

I can't de - ny____ what I be - lieve;____

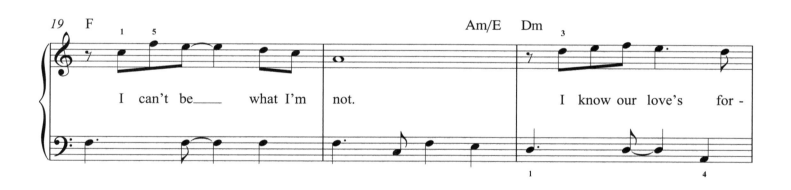

I can't be____ what I'm not. I know our love's for -

- ev - er, I know no mat - ter what.____

Oh, Pretty Woman

Words & Music by Roy Orbison & Bill Dees

'She walked off the street, into his life and stole his heart' ran the coy tagline to this 1990 story of a prostitute with a nice smile. Roy Orbison's pounding 1964 hit was dusted off to give Julia Roberts' dazzling breakout performance a film title and a tune.

Hints & Tips: You will add to the rhythmic effectiveness of this song if you take care to hold the left-hand crotchets (quarter notes) for their exact length.

wo - man____ won't you par - don me,____ Pret - ty wo - man____ I could-n't

help but see,____ Pret - ty wo - man____ that you look

love - ly as can be, Are you lone - ly just like

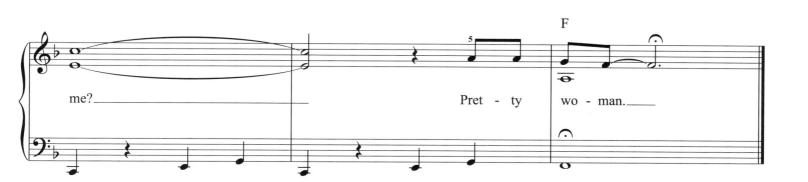

me?____ Pret - ty wo - man.____

Raindrops Keep Falling On My Head

Words by Hal David • Music by Burt Bacharach

This is the landmark song that launched the practice of putting pop songs into movies. Traditional film score composers were outraged, but in the end it turned out there was room for both, and the movie soundtrack album really took off.

Hints & Tips: This song has a gentle swing feel to it. Keep your playing nice and relaxed.

The Killers
Read My Mind

Words & Music by Brandon Flowers, Dave Keuning, Mark Stoermer & Ronnie Vannucci

This Las Vegas-based rock band's lead vocalist Brandon Flowers deemed this the best song he'd ever written. It was widely praised, despite negative reviews for their album *Sam's Town*, from which it was the third of four tracks to be released as a single in the UK, NME describing it as a 'righteous and anthemic album highlight'.

Hints & Tips: Emphasise the first crotchet of eight (spread over two bars) to prevent this arrangement sounding monotonous and boring. Also bring out the chords (bars 10–11 and 14–16) and motifs (bars 26–27 and 30–31) that feature between the phrases to create extra interest.

Rocket Man

Words & Music by Elton John & Bernie Taupin

This song was ranked at No. 242 in Rolling Stone magazine's 500 Greatest Songs Of All Time. The lyrics concern a man who is evidently about to depart for Mars as an astronaut, and is anxious that he will miss his family. It has been covered by many other artists, including Kate Bush.

Hints & Tips: This song has a complex and varied vocal line. The right hand imitates this, and if you find the rhythm tricky, try marking in the beats of each bar with a pencil. This should help you to fit the semiquaver rhythms with the left-hand part. The left hand stays quite still, so practise this first until it is secure.

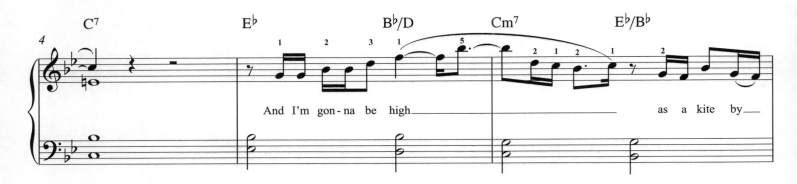

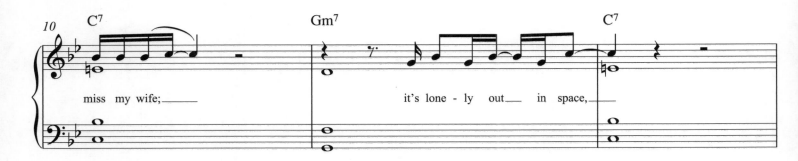

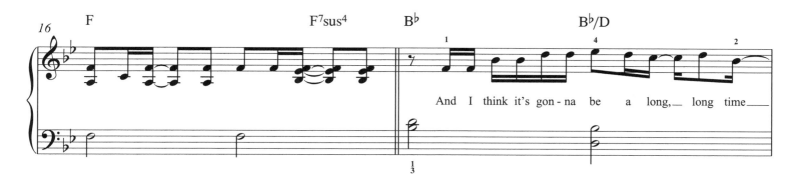

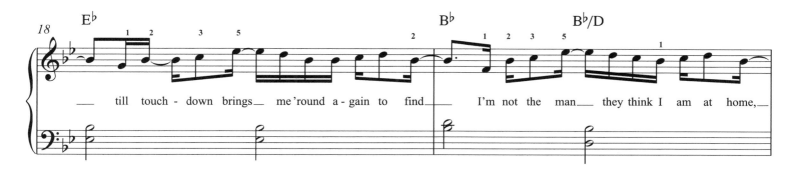

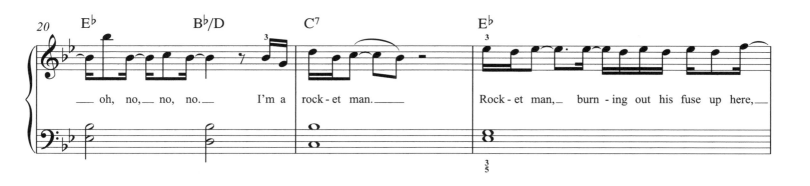

FRANK SINATRA
Strangers In The Night
Words by Charles Singleton & Eddie Snyder • Music by Bert Kaempfert

This song featured in the 1957 movie The Joker Is Wild, the true story of nightclub singer Joe E. Lewis, whose vocal chords were damaged by gangsters causing him to rebuild his career as a stand-up comedian. Despite Sinatra croaking his way through, it won that year's Academy Award for Best Original Song.

Hints & Tips: There are a few occasions in this piece when you will need to cross your index finger over your thumb in order to achieve a smooth melodic line, e.g. the right hand in bar 15, and the left hand in bars 8, 24 and 32. Practise this until you are comfortable with it.

ABBA
Super Trouper

Words & Music by Benny Andersson & Björn Ulvaeus

ABBA's last British No. 1 has the distinction of being the only song containing the word 'Glasgow' ever to top the UK charts. Another thumping anthem with a percussive lyric, it still has 'hit' written all over it.

Hints & Tips: Notice that the two halves of this piece are very similar.
Always count a regular beat when you play music, this will help you play the correct rhythms.

EURYTHMICS

Sweet Dreams (Are Made Of This)

Words & Music by Annie Lennox & Dave Stewart

It is said that Dave Stewart of Eurythmics came up with the bass line to this tune after playing the music from a music box backwards! The video for the song famously featured Annie Lennox dressed as both a woman and a man.

Hints & Tips: If you are not familiar with playing in C minor, check the key signature carefully, and work out which notes are flattened. The bass line is a two-bar pattern repeated throughout.

RIHANNA

Take A Bow

Words & Music by Mikkel Eriksen, Tor Erik Hermansen & Shaffer Smith

The Bajan pop princess's velvety piano ballad about a deceiving partner was written for the re-release of her album *Good Girl Gone Bad* and became her third US No. 1 single by jumping 52 places to the top of the Billboard Hot 100, whilst in the UK it debuted at No. 2 on downloads alone, rising to No. 1 the next week.

Hints & Tips: The right-hand part in bars 9 and 11 requires the third finger to cross-over the thumb. Move the third finger as you have finished playing the F such that it is positioned and ready to play the C when required rather than leaving it to the last minute. Do the same with the thumb when moving between the D and the A.

Viva La Vida

Words & Music by Guy Berryman, Jon Buckland, Will Champion & Chris Martin

The second track to be released as a single from Coldplay's long-awaited fourth album of the same name, its title inspired by a painting by Mexican artist Frida Kahlo, this song gave them their first ever UK No. 1 single in June 2008 when they were also the first British group to reach the top of the US Billboard Hot 100 since 1997.

Hints & Tips: This piece should be played with strong fingers, but that doesn't mean that you should get tense. Keep your fingers relaxed and feel the full weight of them sink into the keys as you play.

For some rea - son I can't___ ex - plain,___ once you'd gone there was

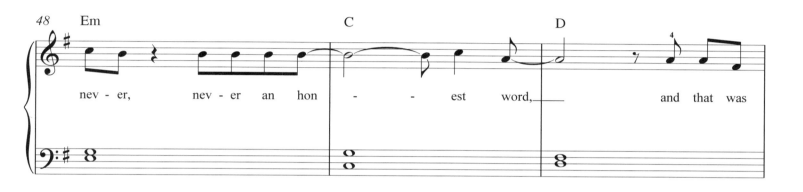

nev - er, nev - er an hon - - est word,___ and that was

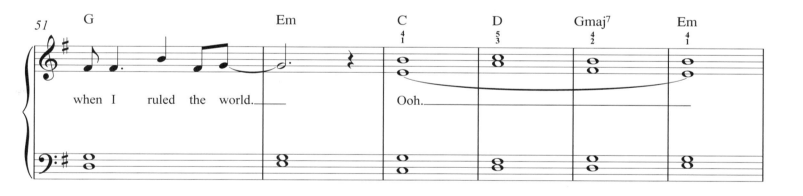

when I ruled the world.___ Ooh.___

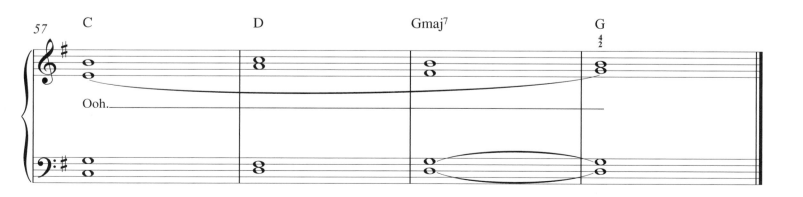

Ooh.___

ABBA
Waterloo

Words & Music by Benny Andersson, Stig Anderson & Björn Ulvaeus

The legendary breakout song with which four oddly dressed Swedes won The Eurovision Song Contest in 1974. One critic said the hook line of 'Waterloo' stayed with you like a kick in the knee, but everyone else knew the song marked the start of something special.

Hints & Tips: Play the chorus of this song with a bright strong beat, taking care with the mixtures of dotted and non-dotted notes, which appear in both hands.

A Whole New World

Words by Tim Rice • Music by Alan Menken

Tim Rice took over as lyricist for this film, based on the Arabian folktale Aladdin's Wonderful Lamp from One Thousand and One Nights, when Disney regular Howard Ashman died in early 1991. In 1993 this became the first Disney song ever to reach No. 1 on the US Billboard Hot 100.

Hints & Tips: Take note that the key signature is F major, which means there are B♭s to remember. Also notice that the left hand has important material as well as the right hand so try to bring this out, e.g. bars 10 and 18.

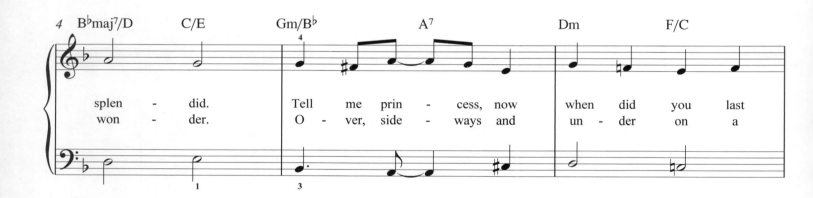

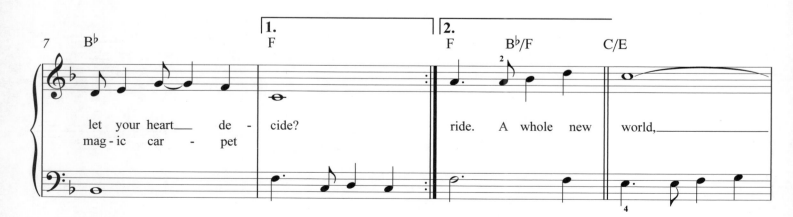

Woke Up This Morning

Words & Music by Chester Burnett, Robert Spragg, Jake Black, Piers Marsh & Simon Edwards

Alabama 3 is an eight-piece band from Brixton, a vibrant, unreconstructed area of London. Despite the band's English roots, the show's producers must have recognised that their music is heavily influenced by American musical styles including blues, country and gospel. 'Woke Up This Morning' has elements of each of these styles woven into a portentous, throbbing acid house groove that reflects the dark and malevolent world of a New Jersey Mafia family.

Hints & Tips: Some of the rhythms are very tricky. Try saying or singing the words to help you—the words are almost spoken in the song and so the rhythms are close to speech patterns.

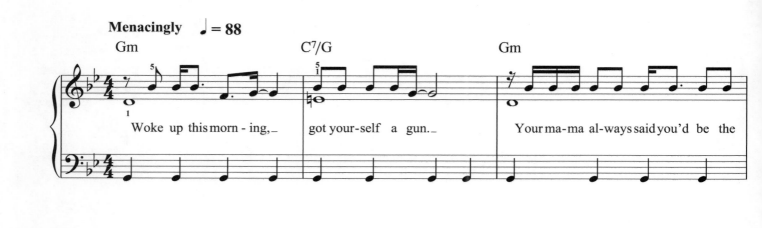

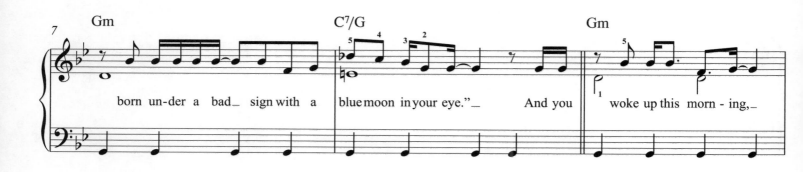

You're Beautiful

Words & Music by Sacha Skarbek, James Blunt & Amanda Ghost

'You're Beautiful' accomplished a feat rarely seen on the modern UK Singles Chart by climbing to No. 1 having initially entered it outside the Top Ten. With it ex-soldier Blunt also became the first British artist to top the American Billboard Hot 100 since Elton John's Candle In The Wind 1997.

Hints & Tips: Play this piece very smoothly (legato) by keeping your fingers close to the keys.

JOHN TRAVOLTA & OLIVIA NEWTON-JOHN

You're The One That I Want

Words & Music by John Farrar

With nine weeks at No. 1 in the UK from 17 June 1978, this was the first of two No. 1 hits these artists had together, the second, 'Summer Nights', topping the charts for seven weeks later the same year. Both were taken from the film Grease, set in the fictional Rydell High School and both also topped the USA's Billboard Hot 100.

Hints & Tips: Make sure you allow the rests in the left hand (of which there are many!) to last for their full value. It is easy to rush these gaps between notes so use a metronome to help you keep the tempo constant.

FROM DISNEY'S 'TOY STORY'

You've Got A Friend In Me

Words & Music by Randy Newman

Composer Andy Newman established his trademark Pixar Animation Studios sound in this 1995 film about the secret life toys lead when people are not around, in particular that of cowboy Woody and Buzz Lightyear, a space ranger. It was the first full-length feature film to use only computer-generated imagery.

Hints & Tips: Play this piece with a gentle swing to capture the laid-back feel of the song, but don't become too relaxed—there are plenty of accidentals to keep an eye out for!

ABBA
Thank You For The Music

Words & Music by Benny Andersson & Björn Ulvaeus

Andersson and Ulvaeus were already harbouring ambitions to write a musical long before Chess. This song, with its lengthy solo vocal introduction, came from their 'mini-musical' The Girl With The Golden Hair.

Hints & Tips: Try and add a swing to the chorus ('Thank You For The Music...') of this song. Be sure to take extra care with the many accidentals in the piece.

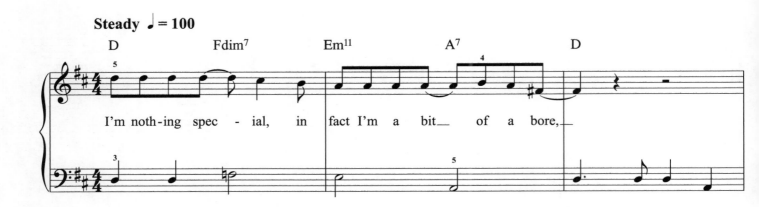

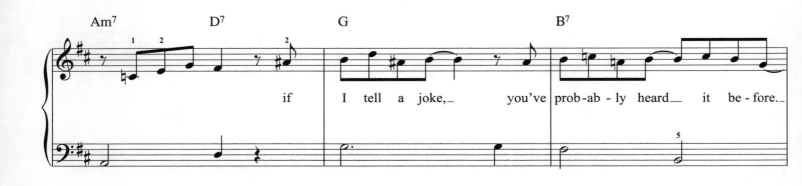

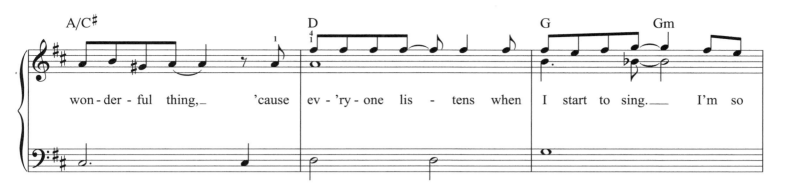

won-der-ful thing,___ 'cause ev-'ry-one lis - tens when I start to sing.___ I'm so

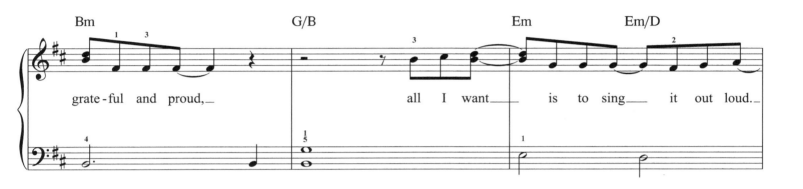

grate-ful and proud,___ all I want___ is to sing___ it out loud.___

___ So I say thank you for the mus - ic the songs I'm sing - ing,

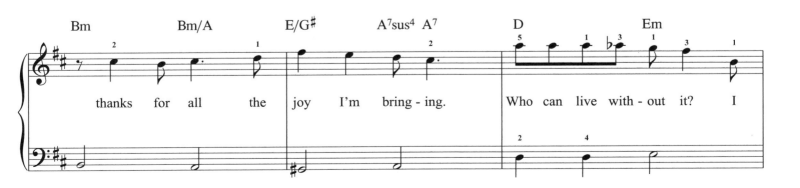

thanks for all the joy I'm bring - ing. Who can live with - out it? I

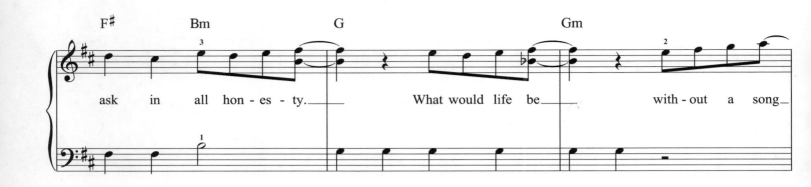

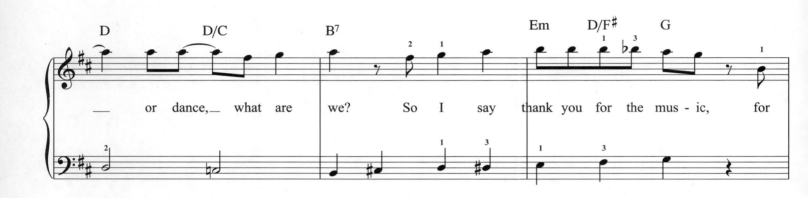

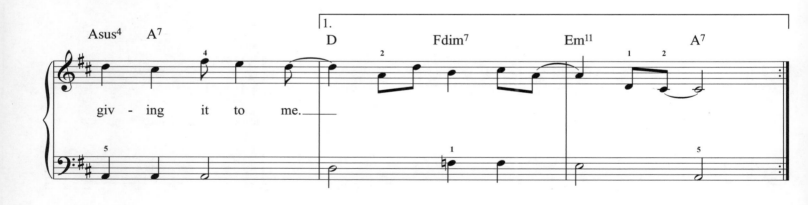

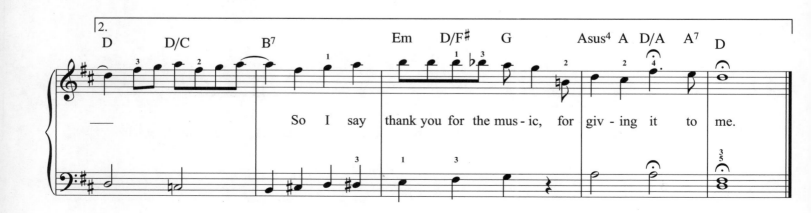